STEAM JOBS FOR

THRILL SEEKERS

BY SAM RHODES

raintree
a Capstone company — publishers for children

Raintree is an imprint of Capstone Global Library Limited, a company incorporated in England and Wales having its registered office at 264 Banbury Road, Oxford, OX2 7DY – Registered company number: 6695582

www.raintree.co.uk
myorders@raintree.co.uk

Text © Capstone Global Library Limited 2019
The moral rights of the proprietor have been asserted.

Lauren Dupuis-Perez, editor; Sara Radka, designer; Kathy McColley, production specialist

ISBN 978 1 4747 6409 4 (hardback)
22 21 20 19 18
10 9 8 7 6 5 4 3 2 1

British Library Cataloguing in Publication Data
A full catalogue record for this book is available from the British Library.

Acknowledgements
Getty Images: AF-studio, background, Antagain, 15 (smoke), Beboy_ltd, 7 (bottom), Charley Gallay, 17, David McNew, 29 (top), Eureka_89, 9 (top), EyeEm, 14, Fuse, 15 (firecrackers), kali9, 19, Marco Di Lauro, 11 (bottom), mikeuk, 7 (top), monkeybusinessimages, 18, Vasilvich, 28 (bottom), yozks, 11 (top); NASA: 22, 23, 24 (bottom), 24 (top), 25; Newscom: Ingram Publishing, 13 (top), Marco Simoni/Robert Harding, 8, Michael Runkel/robertharding, 6, Minden Pictures/Mark Moffett, 12, Photoshot, 13 (bottom), Polaris/David Ryder, 28 (top), Rapport Syndication/Detroit News/David Guralnick, 16, World History Archive, 9 (bottom), ZUMA Wire/Maxppp/Julien De Rosa, 10, ZUMA Wire/Planet Pix/Sean Furey, 27, ZUMA Wire/Planet Pix/Sra Jacob Morgan, 26; NOAA: 20, 21 (bottom); Pixabay: FelixMittermeier, cover (background), 1; Shutterstock: Castleski, cover (astronaut); U.S. Air Force: Tech. Sgt. Kit Thompson, 21 (top); USDA: David Kosling, 29 (bottom), U.S. Forest Service: Kari Greer, 4

Every effort has been made to contact copyright holders of material reproduced in this book. Any omissions will be rectified in subsequent printings if notice is given to the publisher.

All the Internet addresses (URLs) given in this book were valid at the time of going to press. However, due to the dynamic nature of the Internet, some addresses may have changed, or sites may have changed or ceased to exist since publication. While the author and publisher regret any inconvenience this may cause readers, no responsibility for any such changes can be accepted by either the author or the publisher.

Printed and bound in India.

CONTENTS

INTRODUCTION
JOBS ON THE EDGE

Fire conditions can change unexpectedly, so a firefighter needs to be able to think quickly and act fast to avoid danger.

Thrill seekers push themselves to their limits. They like to face challenges. They push their minds and bodies to extremes and take risks in high-action sports or hobbies. Sometimes they even risk death. Thrill seekers make lightning-fast decisions. Then they take action. This is when they are at their best. But thrill seeking can be more than just a hobby. This passion and mindset also leads people to many important careers.

Some of the world's most intense jobs are in STEAM-related fields. STEAM stands for science, technology, engineering, the arts and maths. A strong education is needed. But the benefits can be huge. STEAM jobs are in demand and on the rise. In recent years the number of STEAM jobs has grown at least twice as fast as other careers.

Some STEAM jobs are a good fit for thrill seekers. From exploring a volcano to travelling to outer space, STEAM jobs take thrill seekers to the edge. Discover what the average workday is like for people in these exciting fields.

CHAPTER 1
VOLCANOLOGISTS

AN ERUPTING SCIENCE

At the top of a mountain, an orange glow lights up the sky. The earth below rumbles and shakes. Nearby a fiery lake of lava bubbles and spits. Suddenly hot lava begins to pour out of the top of the Erta Ale volcano in Ethiopia. Dr Lorraine Field went to study this volcano, but she didn't think it would be erupting. She and her team got away. They were lucky. An active volcano is one of the most destructive natural forces on Earth.

The Erta Ale volcano in Ethiopia is one of only a few volcanoes in the world with a permanent lava lake.

A volcanologist is a person who studies volcanoes. The best way to study a volcano is to get really close to it. Volcanologists study the movement of lava underground using special cameras. They also examine **satellite** images to see if big changes are happening in the area.

If they think a volcano is safe, volcanologists will visit it. They quickly take samples of rocks and air. The rocks give volcanologists a look at the **geology** of the area. Volcanologists use a special machine called a mass spectrometer to find out the age of the rock. Volcanologists might collect air samples from volcanic vents. Gases leaking out from these vents give the volcanologists an idea of what is happening deep underground.

After they take their samples, volcanologists return to a laboratory to continue their work. They inspect their samples and write research papers on their findings. Precise predictions for volcanic activity are impossible to make. Volcanologists hope to one day collect enough information to fully predict volcanic eruptions around the world.

EDUCATION

Volcanologists should have a strong background in the following STEAM subjects:

- **geology**
- **earth science**

satellite spacecraft that circles Earth; satellites gather and send information

geology study of minerals, rocks and soil

Volcanologists chip off different mineral samples using a rock hammer. The samples are then studied in a lab.

THE RIGHT TOOLS FOR THE JOB

Studying active volcanoes is difficult. Just getting to volcanoes is a tough job. Volcanoes aren't usually found near cities or paved roads. Volcanologists often must hike through remote jungles or climb cold mountains to get to work.

On the volcano, scientists use special equipment to stay safe. Gas masks provide protection to scientists while they work around vents. Volcanologists also wear hard hats to protect themselves from falling rocks.

STEAM FACT

A man called Pliny the Younger is thought to be the first volcanologist. He documented the eruption that destroyed Pompeii, Italy, in AD 79.

In addition to safety equipment, these scientists use a variety of tools to take and record measurements. They use special instruments to measure the different gases that a volcano emits. Seismometers measure the way the ground shakes before a volcanic eruption. Volcanologists use **GPS** to map the ground around a volcano. They often bring notebooks, laptops, or tablets to take notes and record measurements. Volcanologists also take pictures and videos to document volcanic activity.

MOUNT ST HELENS

Mount St Helens in Washington state erupted suddenly the morning of 18 May 1980. It was the worst volcanic eruption in US history. The eruption killed 57 people. Volcanologist David A. Johnston was among the victims. He had been camped on the side of the volcano. He knew the eruption was close and was taking measurements. The eruption destroyed more than 200 homes. During the eruption, 1.25 cubic kilometres (0.3 cubic miles) of ash shot into the sky. This amount would fill 500,000 Olympic swimming pools with ash.

GPS electronic tool that uses satellites to find the location of objects; GPS stands for Global Positioning System

CHAPTER 2
WAR PHOTOJOURNALISTS

An entire city street lies in ruin. The air is thick with concrete dust. People gather, numbly looking through the wreckage of the bombing.

Scenes like this one have played out in many countries throughout history. War photojournalists bring people's attention to war zones. They take pictures of soldiers and **civilians** caught up in the conflicts.

Photojournalists in war zones face many dangers themselves. They can be kidnapped. Enemy soldiers are always a threat. Mines and other unseen explosives can also harm them.

Photojournalists in war zones often provide their own safety equipment, such as helmets and bulletproof vests.

Modern SLR Camera

War photojournalists must have technological skills. Modern cameras have many settings. These settings affect the final images. Shutter speed is very important. It affects how much light goes through the camera. Photojournalists must pick the right lens for the job too. Standard lenses offer a view similar to what the human eye sees. A wide-angle lens captures landscapes well. A zoom lens makes objects that are many metres away look close.

Photojournalists must also use their artistic skills to edit pictures. They use photo editing software. They can retouch pictures to remove flaws. They may also lighten or darken the image. When used well, these changes help the photograph tell the intended message.

EDUCATION

Photojournalists should have a strong background in the following STEAM subjects:

- **visual art**
- **photography**
- **computer science**

civilian person who is not in the military

CHAPTER 3

HERPETOLOGISTS

Deep in the Amazon rainforest, the air feels humid and thick. A team of scientists trudge through the **undergrowth**. They are looking for the green anaconda, the largest snake in the world. The calls of birds and monkeys are beautiful. But they are also unsettling. They remind the scientists that they are in a jungle. Wild animals are all around them. They must tread carefully.

Herpetologists often find themselves in situations like this. Herpetologists study reptiles and **amphibians**. They study some of the most dangerous animals in the world. These animals include snakes, crocodiles, alligators and frogs. Herpetologists usually work for governments, universities, zoos, or museums. They often work to protect **threatened** animals.

There are more than 18,000 species of reptiles and amphibians for herpetologists to study.

Many herpetologists do field work. They travel to distant locations to study animals. Field work can last several weeks or months at a time. During field work, herpetologists can come into contact with stinging insects, dangerous animals and rough terrain.

Field work includes catching animals to study them. Special tools are used to keep the animal and the researcher safe. They include nets, snake pinners and traps. Herpetologists must then handle each animal very carefully. They must avoid being bitten, scratched, or poisoned. Herpetologists measure an animal's weight and length. They also take photos. They want to see how animals are affected by outside events. Pollution, disease and climate change can be problematic for animals.

EDUCATION

Herpetologists should have a strong background in the following STEAM subjects:

- **biology**
- **conservation science**
- **advanced maths**

undergrowth shrubs, small trees and other plants that grow below large trees in a forest

amphibian cold-blooded animal with a backbone; amphibians live in water when young and can live on land as adults

threatened in danger of dying out

CHAPTER 4
PYROTECHNICIANS

Millions of kilograms of fireworks can be set off during big celebrations.

FIRED UP!

No big celebration is complete without fireworks. The people behind those displays are pyrotechnicians. Pyrotechnicians design and put on large firework shows. All fireworks owe their brilliance to chemistry. In other words, the process of making fireworks is strictly science.

Pyrotechnicians work in labs. They mix chemicals that will react when **detonated**. Different chemicals create different coloured explosions.

But before they can explode, the fireworks have to get into the sky. Lift charges are the first explosions to go off. They propel the fireworks into the air. Pyrotechnicians can adjust the height of the fireworks. They do this by changing the strength of the lift charge. The fuses are also timed. Each firework detonates at a specific moment.

STEAM FACT

The Guinness World Record for largest fireworks display was set in the Philippines in 2016. In just 1 hour, 810,904 fireworks were set off.

A pyrotechnician's job is fun, but it can be very risky. Working with large amounts of explosives is dangerous. A stray spark could cause a large explosion. People can get hurt or killed. That's why safety is the number-one concern for pyrotechnicians. Pyrotechnicians wear special clothes and equipment. These help protect workers' skin and eyes from burns. Pyrotechnicians also use computers to launch firework displays. **Automation** reduces the possibility of human error and makes the display safer.

detonate to cause something to explode

automation process of running machines by using computers rather than people

PYROTECHNICIANS ON SET

Gunshots ring out. The hero is pinned down behind a car. She is running out of time. With one bullet left, the hero is desperate. Then something catches her eye. A tank of petrol. It's her only hope. She leaps from behind the car and fires her final bullet. The tank erupts into a ball of flames. Filmgoers watching this action unfold are filled with excitement and suspense.

Pyrotechnicians often use TNT to make large film explosions, which can last as long as seven seconds!

Explosions happen often in films. Pyrotechnicians are the ones who create them. They start by planning the explosion. It must be controlled and look impressive. They might use C-4, dynamite, gunpowder, or other explosives. Like fireworks, different explosives create different sizes and shapes. A fireball that flies through a tunnel uses one kind of explosive. A building or a car explosion uses another type.

Once they know which explosives to use, the pyrotechnicians run tests. First they make sure the area is cleared. Everyone must remain a safe distance away. Anyone observing must use protective equipment, such as goggles and earplugs.

Now it is time to film the explosions. Technicians run more tests to account for any new conditions, such as wind, camera locations and requests from the director. Then the director shoots the scene with many cameras from various angles. Throughout the filming, the pyrotechnician ensures that safety measures are followed.

EDUCATION

Pyrotechnicians should have a strong background in the following STEAM subjects:

- **chemistry**
- **physics**
- **visual art**

CHAPTER 5

EMERGENCY MEDICAL TECHNICIANS

EMTs treat millions of people every year.

A siren wails as an ambulance flies through an intersection. Inside the ambulance a victim lies on a stretcher. The emergency medical technician (EMT) inside works to stabilize the patient. A heart attack stopped the patient's heart, but CPR started it again. That was a close call.

While on the job, EMTs must be prepared at all times. EMTs respond to emergency calls. Emergencies include heart attacks and car accidents. EMTs travel in ambulances, helicopters and planes. They are often the first medical workers to arrive at accident scenes. These healthcare workers make split-second decisions. EMTs must be confident in their training. They perform emergency care at the scene, such as first aid and life support. In rural areas, EMTs are especially important. They provide care when hospitals are far away. These medical workers operate lifesaving equipment, including **defibrillators** and **mask resuscitators**. These tools help EMTs keep patients alive while on the way to a hospital.

Upon arrival at a hospital, EMTs report to the doctor. They tell the doctor the condition of the patient. This includes the treatments given and any known allergies. Their knowledge of medicine and the human body saves lives every day.

EDUCATION

EMTs should have a strong background in the following STEAM subjects:

- **physiology**
- **chemistry**
- **anatomy**

defibrillator electronic device that applies an electric shock to restart the heart

mask resuscitator medical device that pushes air into a person's lungs when he or she is not breathing

CHAPTER 6
HURRICANE HUNTERS

The 2017 hurricane season was one of the most active in recent history. In September, hurricanes Katia, Irma and Jose threatened the east coasts of the United States and Mexico.

Most people leave when a hurricane is coming. But hurricane hunters fly planes into these dangerous storms. These scientists want to study the storms up close. These inside looks provide scientists with the most accurate information. Hurricane hunters collect data on wind speed, **air pressure** and more. Their ultimate goal is to help warn people who might be in the paths of the storms.

STEAM FACT

Because people shouldn't parachute in a hurricane, hurricane hunting aeroplanes usually don't have parachutes. The planes do usually carry rafts and life jackets for emergencies.

Hurricane hunters from the US Air Force often fly the WC-130 Hercules into hurricanes.

Once inside a hurricane, scientists release devices called dropsondes. These devices float through the storm. They take readings on air temperature, **humidity** and wind speed. The dropsondes send this information back to the scientists. The dropsondes transmit data until they are eventually destroyed by the storm.

Most veteran hurricane hunters have experienced at least one near-death experience. In 1989 hurricane hunter Dr Frank Marks and other scientists were researching Hurricane Hugo from an aeroplane. Suddenly the plane's radar went dead. The plane was tossed around inside the hurricane for an hour. They couldn't find a way back out. They almost crashed into the ocean before a second plane came to lead them out of the storm.

EDUCATION

Hurricane hunters should have a strong background in the following STEAM subjects:

- **calculus**
- **physics**
- **meteorology**

air pressure weight of air pushing against something

humidity measure of moisture in the air

CHAPTER 7

ASTRONAUTS

UP, UP AND AWAY

Astronauts have a thrilling job blasting out of Earth's atmosphere in rocket-powered shuttles. Whizzing around Earth at 27,350 km (17,000 miles) per hour is just part of the job for these thrill seekers. Astronauts perform important scientific work. In order to make space exploration safer and easier, they learn as much as possible about outer space.

A spacewalk that takes place outside a spaceship is called extravehicular activity.

There are many challenges to space exploration. In outer space there is very little gravity. This is why astronauts float around in their spaceships. The lack of gravity can cause problems for people who are in space for a long time. Astronauts study the effects of **microgravity** on themselves, plants and animals.

Space provides a unique environment to perform many types of experiments. Astronaut scientists study vaccines and bone health. These experiments might improve quality of life on Earth.

Despite many safety measures, space travel remains dangerous. Thousands of things must go exactly right to avoid disaster during **reentry** to Earth's atmosphere. The craft itself must be built to withstand the incredible forces of reentry, including heat and pressure. Despite this, the crew still experiences extreme **g-forces** upon reentry, which can blur vision and cause some people to pass out.

EDUCATION

Astronauts should have a strong background in the following STEAM subjects:

- **calculus**
- **computer science**
- **physics**
- **engineering**

microgravity condition of weightlessness in space

reentry movement of an object from outer space in and through the atmosphere of a planet

g-force force of gravity on a moving object

On Earth a spacesuit weighs about 127 kg (280 pounds). In space it weighs nothing.

LIFE ON THE INTERNATIONAL SPACE STATION

On the International Space Station (ISS), astronauts live in a tight space. Just moving around without bumping into delicate electronics is difficult. Hygiene is a challenge too. Microgravity makes water extremely hard to control. Astronauts use damp towels to bathe. They use non-rinse shampoo. Even eating in space takes practice.

Astronauts usually spend about six months working and living on the ISS. The scientists use the tools on board to take measurements and process data that would be impossible to get from Earth. The living quarters may be uncomfortable, but the work the astronauts do there is very important.

BECOMING AN ASTRONAUT

It takes up to two years of training to become an astronaut. Recruits learn to fly an aircraft. They first practise using flight **simulators**. Once they master the simulations, they begin flying an aeroplane called a T-38. The T-38 is one of the most important training tools for astronauts. It flies at 1,300 km (800 miles) per hour and up to 17,000 metres (55,000 feet) in the air. The pilots experience more than seven times the force of gravity.

Astronaut trainees also prepare for the weightlessness of space. They do this by riding in an aeroplane called the KC-135. NASA designed this plane to fly very high and dive very fast. The diving creates weightless conditions for the passengers. The plane can dive for up to 25 seconds at a time. This plane is also known as the "Vomit Comet" because many people vomit from the intense ride.

Astronaut trainees prepare for space walks by practising in the Neutral Buoyancy Laboratory. Astronauts wear a special suit to float in this pool. The suit is rigged with weights and flotation devices. The rigging makes a person equally able to float or sink. The effect mimics the weightlessness of space.

STEAM FACT

"Astronaut" is the combination of two Greek words, *astro* and *nautes*, which mean "star sailor".

Astronauts may train underwater for up to seven hours a day.

---

simulator device designed to reproduce what actually occurs in reality

CHAPTER 8
EOD TECHNICIANS

The area is clear and quiet. Deadly quiet. The technician's heart races in her chest. She quickly and carefully feels around inside the discarded backpack. Wires, a trigger, explosives – these confirm the technician's fears. It's a bomb. Luckily, she is an expert.

Army EOD technician recruits spend 37 weeks in training.

Explosive ordnance disposal (EOD) technicians are trained to do many dangerous jobs. They defuse bombs. They **neutralize** chemical spills. Sometimes hazardous materials spill or leak. When this happens, EOD technicians will be called. They safely transport and dispose of dangerous materials. Safety is a priority for EOD technicians. But working with explosives and other hazardous items is never completely safe.

EOD technicians work with advanced technological tools to get the job done. They use special remote control robots to disarm bombs. They might also use metal detectors and sensors on their vehicles to find bombs.

Many EOD technicians work in the military. Military EOD technicians have one of the longest training processes. This is because their work is so dangerous. Navy EOD teams have their own training. They must defuse underwater mines. They wear special SCUBA masks for this job. These masks don't produce bubbles like normal masks. Bubbles could activate a mine.

neutralize to stop a threat from being harmful for any longer

EDUCATION

EOD technicians should have a strong background in the following STEAM subjects:

- **algebra**
- **physics**
- **chemistry**

CHAPTER 9
SMOKE JUMPERS

Sometimes wildfires burn in remote areas. If fire engines can't get there, smoke jumpers are called. Smoke jumpers parachute into burning forests. They provide an initial attack on wildfires. Parachuting into a fire area is very dangerous. An unexpected gust of wind can push a parachute into trees or other obstacles. Landing on uneven terrain could cause broken or sprained bones, making a firefighter unable to flee from an oncoming blaze. Smoke inhalation and falling trees are also constant dangers for smoke jumpers.

Once on the ground, smoke jumpers work with chainsaws and axes. They create **fire lines** to keep the fire from spreading. Smoke jumpers cut down anything, from shrubs to huge trees.

STEAM FACT

Deanne Shulman became the first female smoke jumper in 1981.

Smoke jumpers must be able to survive on their own for up to 48 hours. They rely on limited supplies and their knowledge of the forest.

If someone is injured, smoke jumpers provide lifesaving medical care. For this reason, they must have knowledge of emergency medical treatment and first aid.

Smoke jumper teams also plan and manage **prescribed burns** when they aren't being called in for emergencies. They create a burn plan that identifies the best area and method to manage a fire.

EDUCATION

Smoke jumpers should have a strong background in the following STEAM subjects:

- **forestry**
- **environmental science**
- **biology**

fire line area that has been cleared of vegetation or other materials that can fuel a fire

prescribed burn fire set on purpose by firefighters to get rid of dead trees and plants

GLOSSARY

air pressure weight of air pushing against something

amphibian cold-blooded animal with a backbone; amphibians live in water when young and can live on land as adults

automation process of running machines by using computers rather than people

civilian person who is not in the military

defibrillator electronic device that applies an electric shock to restart the heart

detonate to cause something to explode

fire line area that has been cleared of vegetation or other materials that can fuel a fire

geology study of minerals, rocks and soil

g-force force of gravity on a moving object

GPS electronic tool that uses satellites to find the location of objects; GPS stands for Global Positioning System

humidity measure of the moisture in the air

mask resuscitator medical device that pushes air into a person's lungs when he or she is not breathing

microgravity condition of weightlessness in space

neutralize to stop a threat from being harmful for any longer

prescribed burn fire set on purpose by firefighters to get rid of dead trees and plants

reentry movement of an object from outer space in and through the atmosphere of a planet

satellite spacecraft that circles Earth; satellites gather and send information

simulator device designed to reproduce what actually occurs in reality

threatened in danger of dying out

undergrowth shrubs, small trees and other plants that grow below large trees in a forest

FIND OUT MORE

BOOKS

Ground Control to Major Tim: The Space Adventures of Major Tim Peake, Clive Gifford (Wayland, 2017)

International Space Station: An Interactive Space Exploration Adventure (You Choose Books), Allison Lassieur (Raintree, 2017)

Reptiles and Amphibians (DKfindout!) (Dorling Kindersley, 2017)

Volcanologist (The Coolest Jobs on the Planet), Hugh Tuffen with Melanie Waldron (Raintree, 2014)4)

WEBSITES

www.myworldofwork.co.uk/my-career-options/job-profiles
Find out more about the careers you're interested in on this website.

nationalcareersservice.direct.gov.uk
Use this website to get advice about training and careers.

spacecentre.co.uk/blog-post/how-to-be-an-astronaut
This blog from the National Space Centre is all about becoming an astronaut.

INDEX